A brief history

of the yuan renminbi (RMB)

Pascal Rigaud

For Karine and Paul

TABLE OF CONTENTS

INTRODUCTION   5

**I. THE "PEOPLE'S CURRENCY" IN "CHINA   9
RECONSTRUCTS" AND IN NEW CHINA (1948-
1999)**

1. A new monetary and financial order (1948-1954)   11

2. The affirmation of a communist bank (1955-1978)   25

3. Becoming a leading bank in a "socialist market   37
economy" (1978-1999)

**II. THE CURRENCY OF AN EMERGING   43
POWER (1999-2016)**

1. The smiling face of the "Great Helmsman"   44

2. Towards limited exchange rate flexibility   51

3. CNY and CNH, currencies of a reforming communist   59
regime

**III. THE INTERNATIONAL FUTURE AND   63
DIGITAL YUAN (2016 -)**

1. The inclusion of the renminbi (RMB) in the Special   64
Drawing Rights (SDR)

2. The e-yuan, a central bank digital currency (CBDC)   78

3. The renminbi, the tomb of the US dollar?   85

CONCLUSION   93

When at the beginning of 2021, a few months after the experiment in the city of Shenzhen, the inhabitants of Beijing could participate in a great lottery with their mobile phones, they were collaborating in an initiative that would go down in history monetary: the people drawn received a dematerialized **"red envelope"** (红包, hong bao), with the amount of 200 yuan (25 euros),

to use the first **digital renminbi** (数字人民币, shuzi renminbi), online and offline, during the Chinese New Year. These new monetary signs were used between February 10 and 17 in certain stores and restaurants on Wangfujing, one of the capital's main pedestrian shopping streets, or on e-commerce platforms. The country's six major commercial banks were involved in the operation under the supervision of the **People's Bank of China** (中国人民银行, zhongguo renmin yinhang) as well as the major financial technology companies and e-commerce giants who developed digital wallets and other technologies needed to store and transfer the new virtual currency.

The e-yuan was not designed in a "garage" on the edge of the 101 freeway between southern San Francisco and the city of San Jose, or in an air-conditioned open-space of a fintech in Silicon Wadi, the Israeli equivalent of Silicon

Valley, where high-tech industries are concentrated, but in the new buildings of the Zhongguancun district (Beijing), in the north of the country, or those of Shenzhen, in the south, where excellence has affirmed in terms of digital technologies. After Shenzhen (Guangdong) and Suzhou (Jiangsu), Beijing was the third city to test the use of digital yuan by individuals. Since then, trials have multiplied and "pilot projects" have widened and deepened: the use of a digital currency has become a reality for hundreds of millions of Chinese users.

The **yuan** (元) is the monetary unit of the People's Republic of China (PRC). The expression refers to a sinogram, meaning "round object", like the **cash coins** (钱, qian, 方孔钱, fangkong qian), these small round coins with a square hole, which circulated for centuries in imperial China. At the end of the **Qing** dynasty (清, 1636-1912), the word yuan was also used with the term **dollar** (美元) which refers to silver coins, with the figure of a dragon, an imperial symbol, struck on the obverse, having a weight of approximately 27.22 grams and a fineness of 0.900. In Europe, the name of the monetary unit (yuan) is often used to designate the Chinese currency whose proper name is **"people's currency"** or **renminbi** (人民币). The renminbi is the official currency of the People's Republic of China (PRC).

During the first half of the 20th century, China experienced significant monetary changes, illustrating the difficulties of the nationalist regime to impose itself both in the face of foreign occupation, then the Japanese invasion and finally the Communist troops. In contrast to this instability, the renminbi would remain the legal currency of the government led by the Chinese Communist Party (CCP) despite the diversity of economic experiences that the continent has experienced in the second part of the 20th century. It is the same currency and the same monetary authority that accompanied industrial and agricultural collectivism, then the policy of openness and the insertion of the country into liberal globalization. **Chapter 1: "People's Currency" in New China and New China (1948-1999)**

The **People's Republic of China** (PRC) (中华人民共和国, Zhonghua renmin gongheguo) is a centralized state divided into 22 provinces, 5 autonomous regions and 4 autonomous municipalities. The PRC now includes the two Special Administrative Regions (SAR) of Hong Kong and Macau, which each have their own currency, respectively the **Hong Kong dollar** (港元货币, gangyuan huobi) and the **pataca** (澳門圓, aomen yuan). The renminbi is therefore **legal tender** (法定货币, fading huobi) on the continent but not (yet) in the former British and Portuguese colonies. However, it is also by relying on

Hong Kong that the continent has become a commercial power and that the renminbi has become international.

Chapter 2: The Currency of an Emerging Power (1999-2016)

Chinese **financial diplomacy** (金融外交, jinrong waijiao) has imposed its agenda in bilateral or multilateral relations, as illustrated by the inclusion of the renminbi in the reserve assets of the International Monetary Fund (IMF). While the central banks of the major advanced economies are still wondering about the architecture of a currency adapted to digital transformations, the People's Bank of China is the first central bank of a major economic power to adopt a **digital currency** (数字货币, shuzi huobi). This legal alternative to coins and banknotes aims to facilitate the daily lives of Chinese residents, making digital payments easier and safer; it can also become one of the vectors of affirmation of a multipolar international monetary system. **Chapter 3: The international and digital future of the yuan (2016-)**

Chapter 1

THE "PEOPLE'S CURRENCY" IN "CHINA RECONSTRUCTS" AND IN NEW CHINA (1948-1999)

The first issue of the renminbi was released before the creation of the new regime. It was used to stabilize areas controlled by communist troops. Faced with the currencies of the nationalist government, which had lost all credibility with the population, the "people's currency" participated in the victory by becoming the credible currency of a new economic and financial order (**1.**).

Once hyperinflation had been combated, the banking system had to be centralized and rationalized in order to ensure the "socialist development" of the country. Although it was intended to be the only financial institution in a monobank system, the People's Bank of China had to take into account the supervision of the Ministry of Finance and China's specific agricultural characteristics (**2.**).

At the beginning of 1978, the People's Bank of China became a specific administrative entity. It was thus the main architect of the organization of the banking oligopoly which was being set up and allowed it to become the first rank bank which would promote the diversification of credit institutions (**3.**).

1. A new monetary and financial order (1948-1954)

The **People's Bank of China** (中国人民银行, Zhongguo renmin yinhang) was founded on December 1, 1948, in the city of Shijiazhuang (Hebei Province) by the merger of various regional banks: the Bank of Hubei, the Bank of Beihai, and the Northwest Agricultural Bank. **Nan Hanchen** (南汉宸, 1895-1967, governor from 1948 to 1954), who had gained experience in printing and circulating banknotes during the years of the civil war and the struggle against Japan, was appointed general manager of the new structure. He then became one of the main officials of the banking system. He assisted **Chen Yun** (陈云, 1905-1995), future chairman of the Economic and Financial Committee of the central government, who was to guide the early economic policy of the **"China reconstruts"**[1] (中国建设, Zhongguo jianshe).

The **Red Army** (红军, hongjun) was founded by the Chinese Communist Party (CCP) on August 1, 1927 at

---

[1] China Reconstructs (or China construction) was a monthly magazine founded in 1952 and published in multiple languages aimed to promote a positive image of the People's Republic of China outside the country. It was later renamed Modern China then China Today (今日中国, jinri zhongguo).

the beginning of the **Civil War** (1927-1949, 国共内战, hanyu pinyin). After the surrender of Japan (1945), it became the **Chinese People's Liberation Army** (中国人民解放军, zhongguo renmíin jiefang jun), designated by the acronym PLA (People's Liberation Army). The first communist banks were initially intended to finance these armed forces, including seizing the assets of banks in conquered areas and issuing bills, as the scarcity of metal used for military purposes limited the production of coins. The resumption of open conflict with the Nationalist troops, which the Communist authorities referred to as the **"war of liberation"** (解放战争, jiefang zhanzheng), multiplied in the north of the country banks issuing currency signs used to ensure the supply of regional armies.

The first banknotes issued by the People's Bank of China had therefore, first of all, a unifying function. It was a question of bringing together the banking structures in the "zones liberated" by the PLA troops and converting the different currencies issued by the various communist banks. The new currency is also intended to abolish the old monetary order both by replacing the currencies issued under the **Republic of China** (1912-1949, 中华民国, zhonghua minguo) by the banks controlled by the nationalists, with the aim of stopping **hyperinflation**

(恶性通货膨胀, exing tonghuo pengzhang) and bringing back financial stability, and by ousting cash from foreign banks, thus ending nearly 100 years of foreign currency.

Many versions of this first series were emitted, illustrating the difficulties of production of the bills when the new bankers had to often change regions and did not have stability in the supply of materials (paper, ink, etc.). Moreover, the printing of the first denominations was rough and the quality of the paper was mediocre. Thus, there were 62 versions of banknotes in 12 denominations: two types of 1 yuan, four types of 5 yuan, four types of 10 yuan, seven types of 20 yuan, seven types of 50 yuan, ten types of 100 yuan, five types of 200 yuan, six types of 500 yuan, six types of 1000 yuan, five types of 5000 yuan, four types of 10000 yuan, and two types of 50000 yuan.

Note that some denominations were dated from the Republican era since they were printed under this regime[2]. More surprising perhaps were the designs chosen for these bills. Whatever the versions, they presented on the obverse, for the small denominations, agricultural scenes (horse pulling a cart, horses ploughing a field, tractors, harvesters, irrigated fields, shepherds, etc.) and industrial scenes (factories, mines, sawmills, etc.) or infrastructures

---

[2] 2. The People's Republic of China (PRC) would adopt the Gregorian calendar.

or modes of transport (station, viaduct, train, sailboat, steamboat, etc.) and floral symbols on the reverse.

In China, as elsewhere, the banknotes that circulate in the social body carry the messages of the political and monetary authorities. Then, what was surprising was the break with the past monetary compositions of communist administrations. These "idyllic" representations no longer had the profile of the bills of the **Chinese Soviet Republic** (1931-1937, 中华苏维埃共和国, Zhonghua suweiai gongheguo) issued from February 1932, in Ruijin, Jiangxi, by the **National Bank of the Chinese Soviet Republic** (中华苏维埃共和国家银行, zhonghua suwei'ai gongheguo guojia yinhang) led by **Mao Zemin** (毛泽民, 1896-1943), Mao Zedong's second brother, which reproduced Lenin's face, the slogans of the Communist International, or the program of the CCP.

Then, the workers and peasants depicted were no longer exhorting to build **soviets** (苏维埃, suweiai) or to overthrow the feudal order, but were witnessing a happy, modernized set of work. In short, the currency signs no longer incited militant activism, it was to celebrate a new order to a population that was now required to be hardworking.

The first bills put into circulation were 10, 20 and 50 yuan denominations. **Dong Biwu** (董必武, 1886-1975), then president of the People's Government of North China, calligraphed the name of the People's Bank of China on the bills, which initially circulated in the territories "liberated" by the PLA with the bills of the Northeast Bank. After North China, Shandong and Northwest China, the "people's currency" was gradually imposed in the country, following the pace of progress of the PLA soldiers.

When the city of Beijing came under their control on January 22, 1949, the bank's executives followed the troops of the 8th Army to move to the future capital. On February 2, the new bank's presses moved to the former site of the **Central Bank** (中央銀行, zhongyang hinyang) in Xijiaominxiang (Beijing), the former banking district in the late Qing Dynasty and during the Republic of China.

Although the People's Bank of China was focused on price stabilization, other tasks piled up endlessly. From printing and distributing the RMB in the newly conquered areas, to setting up agricultural cooperatives or controlling the branches of nationalist banks (Central Bank, Bank of China, Bank of Communications, Chinese Peasants' Bank, etc.), not to mention the financial management of the troops, etc., the missions grew and the work intensified as the army controlled the major cities in the south. The demands for financial support for the development of industrial and agricultural production also had to be met. In the People's Daily of June 22, 1949, Nan Hanchen stated that "supporting production is the central task of the bank's work". Therefore, foreign exchange and savings had to be transformed into industrial loans and loans for the purchase of agricultural products. And this "collection" required working with law enforcement agencies to combat financial activities that had become illegal (e.g., money changers), organizing seizures of gold, dollars, silver and foreign bank bills. The new monetary authorities also had an educational function, as they had to "help" the executives of private banks who had not fled to familiarize themselves with the financial policies of the new China.

The denominations put into circulation had different names. However, the term **"people's money"** (人民币) would spread from mid-1949. When PLA troops entered Shanghai in May 1949, the **gold yuan**[3] (金元, jinyuan) of the old regime had to be exchanged for the RMB at the rate of 1 per 100000: within a few days, the Communist authorities recovered most of the money in circulation. However, it was not the presence of the

---

[3] The gold yuan is the currency of the Republic of China which came into effect on August 19, 1948 to replace the depreciated fabi yuan. One gold yuan is worth 3 million fabi yuan.

nationalist currency, which had been totally discredited, that posed a problem in imposing the new "people's currency" but the circulation of foreign currency and silver dollars.

With the scarcity of goods, RMB prices soared even faster as goods circulated less with the new currency. Grain, cloth, etc. appeared faster when exchanged for silver coins or American or British bills. But the power was relentless against **financial speculation** (金融投机, jinrong touji) which led presciently to courts, and to expeditious executions, for **manipulating prices** (操纵物价). All currency had to be deposited with the Bank of China in exchange for a certificate of deposit, or directly with the People's Bank of China in exchange for renminbi. These requirements showed that there was still a lot of mistrust of this new "people's currency": "The People's Liberation Army can enter Shanghai, but not the renminbi." a saying likes to assert. It would therefore take a soldier to impose the bill. And the mobilization of the "masses" against speculation would strengthen the base of the new notes, especially since the closure of local banks, the criminalization of commercial exchanges in foreign currencies or precious metals and the multiple arrests of "speculators" accompanied the injunctions to monetary virtue.

Despite the military victory, the battle on the **inflation** (通货膨胀, tong huo peng zhang) front was not yet won. The conversion of cash, the absorption of deposits, the control of issuance, the redemption of bills issued under the **Guomindang** (国民党), even at a rate unfavorable to their holders, failed to limit the rise in prices. More fundamentally, the civil war, deteriorating transportation infrastructure, business closures, shortages, especially of grain, material or coal, etc. accelerated price increases. It is worth noting that since 1937, high inflation has marked the daily life of the Chinese. It may have had favorable effects when economic agents saved little and quickly bought industrial and consumer goods on the market. However, when the flight from money became general and irremediable, when merchants changed prices every hour, when civil servants demanded their salaries in kind or when it became impossible to fix an interest rate, economic life came to a standstill. Hyperinflation had reinforced the contempt of a nationalist regime already discredited for its corruption, carelessness, and military defeats; it must not take hold under the new regime.

Nevertheless, the monetary authorities had to print new denominations with a higher nominal amount: 100, 200, 500 and then 1000, 5000, 10000 and 50000 yuan. Chinese exiles in the colony of **Hong Kong** (香港, xianggang) or the island of **Taiwan** (台湾) then anticipated the same price boom that the nationalist regime experienced especially as the fiscal (tax hike) and wage (labor wage hike) news taken by the communist authorities, not to mention the expeditious trials against the capitalists and other owners, did not encourage the resumption of business in a country where connections were difficult via the railroads, the southern ports were blocked and the economic and financial elites were on the run. With the intensification of the civil war, industry was then moribund. And talk of industrial recovery, possibly followed by ideological recovery sessions, rarely had a direct effect on inflation rates... although it did encourage bank deposits in the new institution among frightened savers.

In addition to these external factors of disorganization, there was also the slow organization of the communist administration. Throughout 1949 and 1950, there were many separate local and sectoral budgets. The authorities had to limit the centrifugal pressures of local officials who restricted the circulation of foodstuffs to avoid shortages in their area of control. In addition to these difficulties in assessing expenditures, there were temptations to turn the "money printing press" to finance local expenditures and satisfy central government injunctions. And, within the State in formation, unity of action was not yet guaranteed. Thus, **Bo Yibo** (薄一波, 1908-2007), the Minister of Finance, gave permission to issue 664 billion yuan in paper money in October 1949 accentuating the sharp depreciation of the yuan and fueling rampant inflation.

On the foreign exchange market, the first denominations of the communist regime seemed to depreciate as quickly as the last nationalist yuan, although in April 1949, the new People's Bank fixed the value of the RMB on a basket of physical goods (flour, cloth, etc.). In May 1949, the Hong Kong dollar was worth 138 yuan. The renminbi yuan, which had not yet been fully disseminated in the south of the country, depreciated rapidly despite the military victories. It took more than 1,000 yuan to obtain a dollar in December 1949 and 3,000 yuan in January 1950. The U.S. embargo and the freezing of communist dollar assets in December 1950 would further weaken the external value of the people's currency. However, the main thing was not these unfavorable exchange rates, which masked the main thing: the communist authorities had introduced a new currency that proved to be a viable currency. Violent means were mobilized, but hyperinflation was avoided.

The People's Bank of China continued to strengthen its grip on the banking system, including the transfers of the managements of Nationalist banks from Shanghai to Beijing, such as the **Bank of China's** （中国银行, zhongguo yinhang). It also needed to clarify its relationship with the political authorities and other administrative entities, both civilian and military, in charge of financial matters. Common accounting standards had to be defined among the various agencies, including ensuring that the bank's accounting was compatible with that of the Ministry of Finance and the future planning administration.

It was not only a question of setting up a national banking system, but also of defending the interests of the new power abroad. And while the geographical boundaries of the bank were quickly established, the limits of its prerogatives were the subject of much discussion. In October 1949, the central government approved its application to establish an insurance company, the **People's Insurance Company of China** (中国人民保险, zhongguo renming baoxian) in Beijing.

On October 1, 1949, the **People's Republic of China** (中华人民共和国, Zhonghua renmin gongheguo) was founded in Beijing. It asserted itself as "a people's democracy that realizes the democratic dictatorship of the people, led by the working class, based on the alliance of workers and peasants and rallying all democratic classes and all Chinese nationalities."

On October 19, 1949, the Central People's Government officially appointed Nan Hanchen as Governor of the People's Bank of China and Hu Jingyuan as Vice

Governor. The law incorporated the People's Bank of China as an organ directly under the central people's government. It was regulated by the **Committee of Finance and Economy** (财政经济委员会, caizheng jingji weiyuanhui) to perform the functions of a state bank, responsible for issuing money, bonds, managing government treasury, financial activities, maintaining financial stability and participating in the restoration and reconstruction of the country.

For the executives of the People's Bank of China, the main monetary challenges are already known. It is necessary to complete the unification of currencies throughout the country, control inflation and finance the construction of the new state.

The **renminb**i (人民币) was the currency of the new regime, although the law did not formalize it until 1969! Its Chinese abbreviation, RMB, composed of the initials of the word RenMinBi or **currency** (币, bi) of the **people** (人民, ren min). The **yuan** (元) is the monetary unit of the renminbi. It is divided into 10 **jiao** (角) and 100 **fen** (分). The term yuan renminbi therefore refers to the monetary unit (yuan) and the currency (renminbi). It is used generically to refer to the currency of the People's Republic of China.

When the regime became official in 1949, the conquered territory did not yet have a unified monetary system. The new banknotes of the People's Bank of China still circulated with the old denominations of the Northeast Bank. In addition, there were still a dozen currencies in circulation in the liberated territories. It was not until two years later that the banks in Manchuria and Mongolia no longer had their own issues and that the specific bills issued in the Xinjiang region (November 1951) were withdrawn from circulation. Although prohibited by the Military Control Commission, foreign currency was still circulating, as many Chinese had hoarded precious metals and foreign banknotes at the approach of the Communist troops. In the south of the country, the latter fulfilled the three functions expected of a currency (unit of account, intermediary for trade, reserve of value) even better than the renminbi. For a few months, among the richest people who would go to Taiwan or the British colony if they could, the Hong Kong dollar was used to count and pay on the mainland. It was not until November 1951, with an exception for Tibet (1957), that the "people's currency" became the only currency used by the citizens of the new People's Republic of China.

The banknotes of this first series would be withdrawn from circulation between April 1 and May 10, 1955. They were referred to as "old money" or "old yuan" because of the exchange rate of 10,000 yuan to 1 yuan of the second series (or "new money"), as the stabilization of the regime went hand in hand with the desire to erase the effects of inflation.

2. The affirmation of a communist bank (1955-1978)

Unification and centralization also affected the banking system. Private banks whose owners had fled to Taiwan, Hong Kong or other countries were dissolved or integrated into new structures. For the few financial elites who remained in the country, the **"United front"** (统战, tongzhan) proposed in 1949 offered for a few months the illusion of shared responsibility between communists and non-communists to ensure economic development. **Public-private partnerships** (公私合营, gongsiheying) then appeared to be a stopgap before discovering that seats on boards of directors offered only meager **dividends** (分红, fenhong) and no decision-making power and that the banking system was not intended to escape the socialization of the means of production.

If the government still tried to seduce a few bankers, it was to recover the assets of the banks' subsidiaries abroad or attract the funds of overseas Chinese, but there was, at that time, no more room for a private bank in "a people's democracy that realizes the democratic dictatorship of the people." The centralization of the banking system was aided by the nationalist reforms, which had strengthened state intervention in credit institutions since 1935. Chinese private banking was atrophied under the Guomindang and disappeared under the CCP when the institutions were "socialized" in December 1952. The foreign banks that had not fled disappeared: there were only two American banks after the proclamation of the People's Republic of China. In rural areas, credit cooperatives were created.

At the beginning of 1951, all new credit activities were captured by the new People's Bank. Generally speaking, the enterprises of the "free capitalist sector" represented less than 20% of industrial production in 1952, compared to more than 55% in 1949. And their share was bound to decrease. For the time being, only small businesses escaped state control, but not fiscal and ideological pressures. But very quickly, a quasi-monobank system was established. In August 1955, all banks had to transfer their management, accounting and assets to the People's Bank of China. A year later, the private banking sector no longer existed. Moreover, in 1956, even small traders, street vendors and craftsmen "asked" to join the socialist society...

In September 1949, the law had integrated the People's Bank of China with the administrations directly under the central people's government. And, it was also attached to the Committee of Finance and Economy. The model of the new economic elites was that of a **single-**

bank system (单一银行系统, danyi yinhang xitong) (1948-1978), which, on the Soviet model, would control all money flows in the economy in order to check their compliance with the planning guidelines. In spirit, the People's Bank of China was an administrative department of the Ministry of Finance, and the latter was responsible for central planning, i.e., for setting all prices, including interest rates, and quantities, i.e., for credit flows. It would remain one of the administrative machineries dominated by the Ministry of Finance until 1978.

In practice, one had to take into account the reluctance of certain members of the political bureau to delegate all economic, monetary and financial powers to a single ministry and, above all, the constraints imposed on the government to improve the financing of a rural society that was at once the most numerous social group, the foundation of the army and the heart of Maoist ideology. Thus, the internal struggles to define the respective fields of action of the new bank and the new ministry remained intense.

The **Ministry of Finance** (财政部, caizheng bu) directly controlled the People's Bank for Construction, an institution specializing in priority planning operations that was mainly used to finance basic industry, and the **Bank of Communications** (交通银行股份有限公司, jiaotong yinhang gufen youxian gongsi), placed under his leadership on May 1, 1952, to integrate the objectives of planning and manage the collection of dividends paid to the capitalists who remained in the territory. It would finance, in collaboration with Soviet experts, infrastructure construction work, particularly under the first **Five-Year Plan** (五年计划, wunian jihua) (1953-1957) focused on heavy industry.

Taking over part of the assets of the Bank of Communications, the **People's Construction Bank of China** (中国人民建设银行, zhongguo renmin jianshe yinhang, CCB) was established on May 10, 1954, after the launch of the 1st Five Year Plan (1953-1957). It is an office of the Ministry of Finance that allocated resources to building companies.

The example of the Bank of Communication highlights the hesitation in the constitution of the monobank system. Moreover, in the banking field, the new regime's indecisions to "wipe the slate clean" remained numerous. If it wanted to liquidate the capitalists, both figuratively and literally, the government needed the "collaboration of class enemies" in many areas, especially in banking. Moreover, it would discover that the monobank system was not well adapted to the particularities of financing peasant activities.

The branches of the People's Bank of China formed, a priori, a geographical network better adapted to these challenges. Indeed, the "people's bank" was organized around two distinct circuits: that of fiduciary money, coins and banknotes, which were withdrawn/deposited at the counters intended for individuals; and that of scriptural money, in the form of lines of credit, managed by the counters reserved for enterprises and administrations. Although formally under the supervision of the Ministry of Finance, the People's Bank of China defended its specific financing channels through separate banks:

- the **Bank of China** (BOC), which was gaining increasing weight in financial activities with foreign countries. In 1952, the Foreign Affairs Bureau of the People's Bank of China was merged with the BOC, which was authorized to specialize in foreign exchange activities under the direction of the new monetary authority;

- the **Mixed Bank** created "at the request of about 60 private banks to help them in the course of socialist transformation";

- the **Credit cooperatives**, which were essentially established in rural areas to manage the deposits and loans of peasants. These various credit, supply and marketing cooperatives were to participate in the networking of the rural population.

These boundaries were relatively stable, except for the financing of rural activity. After hesitations to create dedicated banks, the **Agricultural Cooperative Bank** (1952) or the **Agricultural Bank of China** (1954), the Department of Rural Finance of the People's Bank created in 1957 to manage rural financial activities making the People's Bank of China a "super agricultural bank". It was therefore not neutral that the logo of the People's Bank of China is composed of three "spade currencies" linked by their feet. These **monetary spades** (铲币, chan bi) refer to a founding era of imperial China, an agrarian society par excellence, but also, for the Chinese eye, to a more formal reading since the shape of a "人", which appears around and inside the logo, is the stylized writing of the pinyin character "ren" which means "man" or "human being". The multiplication of these "ren" can thus evoke the **"people"** (人民, renmin) that is central to the name and mission of the **People's Bank of China** (中国人民银行, zhongguo renming yinhang).

The second series of RMB was put into circulation on March 1, 1955. It included 11 denominations (1, 2, 5, 10, 20, 50 jiao and 1, 2, 3, 5 and 10 yuan). To ease the circulation of currency, three kinds of coins (1, 2 and 5 jiao) were minted for circulation from December 1, 1957. On the reverse side of the banknotes, the phrase "People's Bank of China" and the name of the banknote was written in Uyghur, Tibetan and Mongolian languages[4]. For the anecdote, this second series of RMB would be the only one to include 3-yuan banknotes.

The 1-yuan and 5-yuan banknotes would be subject to design adjustments in the early 1960s. As the PRC had not yet broken ties with its Russian neighbor, the highest denomination notes (3, 5 and 10 yuan) were printed in the Soviet Union to take advantage of newer printing techniques.

The disagreements between Mao Zedong (1893-1976) and Nikita S. Khrushchev (1894-1971), which emerged after the 20th Congress of the CPSU (1956), were to widen to include the ideological question of the world communist movement and, more prosaically, territorial issues. Mutual denunciations of "revisionism", tensions in international conferences, border incidents (Kyrgyzstan, the Amur and Ussuri rivers, etc.) did not seem, at first, to challenge the active cooperation between the two countries, particularly in the military (cf. the Korean War), nuclear (power plants, submarines, bombs, etc.) or monetary fields. When the People's Daily published from April 1960 a series of articles for the 90th anniversary of Lenin's birth accusing the leadership of the Communist Party

---

[4] There was no inscription in zhuang yet because this alphabet had not yet been standardized.

of the Soviet Union (CPSU) of lacking revolutionary zeal in the Third World, the **Sino-Soviet quarrel** (中苏世仇, zhong su shichou) was brought to light. It resulted, among other things, in the choice of the former "big Soviet brother" to recall, in July 1960, the 1600 Soviet advisers. This radical gesture put an end to a long decade of cooperation since Soviet engineers and specialists had been present since 1948[5]. The withdrawal also led to the cancellation or slowing down of more than 250 cooperation projects. This "quarrel" also resulted in the printing of counterfeit 3, 5 and 10 yuan notes issued by the Soviets to destabilize the Chinese economy, especially in the west of the country, confirming that the currency could become a weapon like any other. The 1953 series of banknotes printed in the USSR were withdrawn from circulation in 1964 (the other series had a longer life).

These destabilization operations remained circumscribed because the "people's currency" had become established in the country. Moreover, banknotes were not the only instruments of exchange in the new China. The war economy, the economic and social weight of the army, the formation of industrial groups and the implementation of planning from 1953 onwards led to the widespread use of

---

[5] The first 300 engineers and specialists arrived in 1948, under the leadership of General Ivan Vladimirovich Kovalev (1901-1993), a specialist in road and rail transport, to support the new technical elites of the regime.

supply vouchers (供应券, gongying quan or 供应票证, gongying piaozheng) for flour, cloth and other certificates for the purchase of charcoal or food, which were often separated for urban and rural people. These various vouchers were all rights of claim that become de facto the second currency in circulation, although they did not circulate throughout the social body and their legality was geographically circumscribed. Some urban households were to depend on the issuance of these booklets and tickets, linked to the registration system of their residence, to ensure their basic purchases (cereals, cooking oil, etc.). Because they were one of the vectors of social control or because they allowed state-owned enterprises to favour their employees, many of these vouchers did not disappear from Chinese economic life until forty years later, in the 1990s.

The Chinese financial system in 1955 must therefore be thought of as a double circuit. A double circuit of monetary signs: the RMB for the people and the coupons for the clientele favored by the government. Double administrative circuit within which, the People's Bank of China operated as a banking administration but under the authority of the Ministry of Finance, which watched over its fiscal and planning prerogatives and which kept the priority in the administrative organization... subject to the arbitration meetings held within the leading bodies of the CCP.

In 1958, the banking system was definitively organized around the People's Bank of China, which had branches throughout the country. It then had five main missions:

- to issue the national currency, the renminbi (RMB) ;
- to grant loans to the economy in accordance with the plan;
- to receive deposits from governments, enterprises, cooperatives and individuals
- manage foreign exchange and international settlements;
- to control and reorganize the various institutions resulting from the absorption of private, mixed and state-owned banks.

The People's Bank of China had become the country's main monetary institution. As both a central bank and a commercial bank, it controlled more than 90% of financial assets and almost all official financial transactions.

The third series of the RMB was put into circulation in April 1962. The banknotes of the second and third series circulated for a while simultaneously (except for the denominations of the year 1953). The dates of issue of the banknotes and the minting of the coins ranged from 1962 to 1980. After the Sino-Soviet breakup, the third series of banknotes was designed and printed only on the territory of the PRC. There are 7 denominations and 13 versions.

Since 1955, the currency signs had conveyed the images of a new modern China: industrialization, mechanization of agriculture, construction, transportation networks, etc. The denominations representing the union of the **workers** (工人, gongren), the **peasants** (农民, nongmin), the **doctors** (医生, yisheng) and the **intellectuals** (知识分子, zhishi fenzi) emphasized the social groups and occupations valued by the power. The ideology printed on the bills remained link to productivism, but it asserted itself more communist. The characters were resolutely modern, confirming the choice of compositions that focused on the socialist construction of the new China: the peasants and educators (1 jiao), the bridge over the Yangtze River (or Blue River) in Wuhan (2 jiao), the textile factory (5 jiao), the peasant woman on her tractor (1 yuan), the lathe worker (2 yuan), and the steel worker in action (5 yuan). The bills thus represented an economy based on agriculture and industry in which industry dominates via the figure of the metal worker, which was found in both the 2 and 5 yuan denominations.

In addition, with this third series, the various **ethnic minorities** (少数民族, shaoshu minzu) were featured along with the members of the National People's Congress (10 yuan). These denominations would be nicknamed the

"Great Unity" (大团结, datuan jie), echoing Mao Zedong's speech of September 30, 1949 entitled "Long Live the Great Unity of the Chinese People" (September 30, 1949). The banknotes of the third series were to be gradually withdrawn from circulation in the mid-1990s before being demonetized on 1 July 2000. This series was therefore distinguished by its duration since they circulated nearly 40 years.

3. Becoming a leading bank in a "socialist market economy" (1978-1999)

On January 1, 1978, the separation between the Ministry of Finance and the People's Bank of China was official. The aim of this separation was to ensure the development of the financial sector in a "planned and progressive" manner within the framework of the policy of economic reform and opening up that had just been initiated.

The new economic orientation of the communist regime was that of a **"socialist market economy"** (社会主义市场经济, shehui zhuyi shichang jingji) based on public ownership "with planning as its guide." This "socialism with Chinese characteristics" resulted, among other things, in the restructuring of the banking system, which gave more freedom to the so-called specialized banks, or commercial banks, which had become more independent of the central bank. Indeed, while liberalization emphasized the efficiency of market mechanisms in the allocation of goods and the creation of **special economic zones** (经济特区, jingji tequ) attracted capital from overseas Chinese and foreigners, the reform of the banking system had to introduce new incentives for all economic agents. Thoughts on the specialization of commercial banks and the level of their independence were therefore driving discussions within the People's Bank of China.

A **central bank** (中央银行, zhongyang yinhang) is, regardless of what it is called (national bank, state bank, people's bank, reserve bank, etc.) the institution whose main function is to issue money and control the amount in circulation. The **People's Bank of China** (中国人民银行, zhongguo renmin yinhang), established on December 1, 1948, would not officially become the country's central bank until 1984 with the passage of its statutes.

From this date, it concentrated on the functions of a modern central bank, its former activities of credits and deposits were essentially managed by the Industrial and Commercial Bank of China (ICBC). Similarly, in the countryside, the Agricultural Bank of China (ABC) extended its activities, especially to merchants. On November 1, 1985, the Industrial and Commercial Bank of China and the Agricultural Bank of China issued their first bonds.

In January 1986, a new regulation on the operation of banks transferred all commercial lending activities from the People's Bank of China to the new "specialized banks" (ABC, BOC, CCB and ICBC), which were initially not responsible for their losses and whose lending activities were not linked to the credit risk of debtors. Other commercial banks were re-established, such as the Bank of Communications (BoCom), or created, such as the Citic Industrial Bank and Everbright Bank.

In the early 1990s, the People's Bank of China was solely responsible for **monetary policy** (货币政策, huobi zhengce) and **supervision of financial institutions** (金融监管机构, jinrong jianguan jigou). The new challenges it had to take on then concerned:

- the transformation of the exchange control system (end of double exchange control);
- the change in the control of banking institutions. Direct control methods, such as credit control or old administrative measures, were being abandoned for indirect control mechanisms via interest rates and reserve requirements;
- the formation of development banks or **"policy banks"** (政策性银行, zhengce xing yinhang) specializing in "political loans" to "free" the four big banks that could fully become commercial banks;
- the opening of the banking industry to foreign institutions.

The banknotes (1, 2, 5 jiao and 1, 2, 5, 10, 50 and 100 yuan) and coins (1 and 5 jiao and 1 yuan) of the fourth series introduced between 1987 and 1997 accompanied the increase in demand for money related to economic development and high growth rates of **gross domestic product** (国内生产总值, guonei shengchan zong zhi).

The preamble to the Chinese Constitution states in its opening lines that "China is one of the oldest countries in the world. Its diverse nationalities, all of whom have contributed to the creation of a brilliant culture, possess glorious revolutionary traditions." It therefore integrates the diversity of the population into one "struggle". The new series thus also responded to the need for political unification of a large and diverse population: "The People's Republic of China is a unitary multinational state, created in common by the various nationalities of the country." (Article 11).

Depending on the criteria chosen (cultural, geographic, linguistic, ethnic, religious, etc.), about 50 groups or more than 200 minorities can be identified (cf. linguistic minorities). As a result of administrative recognition and political (re)construction processes, officially the PRC is composed of 56 ethnicities, nations or **nationalities** (民族, minzu), more than 90% of which are **Hans**[6] (汉族, han zu). Among the hundreds of languages identified in the country, Mongolian, the generic name for

---

[6] The Hans (汉族) are the largest ethnic and cultural group in mainland China and the largest in the world with 18% of the world's population.

languages of the Ural-Altaic family, Tibetan language of the same group as Burmese whose writing is borrowed from northern India, Uyghur spoken in the Xinjiang region, which belongs to the Turkic group of the Altaic language family, and the Zhuang languages spoken in the Guangxi region and neighboring areas (Yunnan, Guangdong, Guizhou, Hunan) are the languages highlighted on the bills. The fourth series celebrates the diversity of the Chinese people through the faces:

- of Miao (苗族) and Manchu (满族) men, 1 jiao;

- of Tujia (土家族) and Korean (朝鲜族) women, 2 jiao;

- of Miao (苗族) and Zhuang (壮族) women, 5 jiao;

- of Dong (东乡族) and Yao (瑶族) women, 1 yuan;

- of Uyghur (维吾尔族) and Yi (彝族) women, 2 yuan;

- of a Tibetan (藏族) and a woman Hui (回族), 5 yuan;

- of Han (汉族) and Mongol (蒙古族) men, 10 yuan;

To this sample of the population, three occupational statuses were added: a worker, a peasant woman and an intellectual (50 yuan cut). Finally, for the largest denomination (100 yuan), the faces in relief of **Mao Zedong** (毛泽东, 1893-1976), **Zhou Enlai** (周恩来, 1898-1976), **Liu Shaoqi** (刘少奇, 1898-1969) and **Zhu De** (朱德, 1886-1976); who are the "four important people for the founding of the People's Republic of China." Note that on the reverse of the 100-yuan bill was reproduced an engraving of the **Jinggang Mountains** (井冈山, jing gang shan), located between Jiangxi and Hunan provinces, which were one of the bases of the Red Army of Workers and Peasants and the "cradle of the Chinese revolution." A poem by Mao, entitled "Mount Jinggang", relates these feats of arms:

" Below the hills fly flags and banners,
Above the hilltops sounds bugles and drums.
The foe encircles us thousands strong,
Steadfastly we stand our ground.
Already our defence is iron-clad,
Now our will unite like a fortress.
From Huangyanggai roars the thunder of cannon,
Word comes the enemy has run away in the night."

This new series reaffirmed the pre-eminence of the historical leaders, who appeared for the first time on the banknotes since the founding of the regime, the economic development and, above all, the unity of all the nationalities making up the Chinese people. In short, it contributed to the construction of a socialism with Chinese characteristics under the leadership of the CCP, which had never failed, even during difficult battles.

The year 1999 saw the introduction of the fifth series of renminbi (RMB). These new denominations were distinguished by the omnipresence of the face of the first president of the People's Republic of China (PRC) on all banknotes (**1.**).

Paradoxically, this monopoly of monetary representation should not obscure the fact that since the death of the "Great Helmsman", the PRC had taken a different path from the one mapped out in the Maoist aspirations. Exchange rate policy had become central in a country which, after joining the World Trade Organization (WTO) in 2001, favored development driven by the integration of companies into liberal globalization (**2.**).

While the PRC's exchange rate regime remained difficult to identify, the internationalization of the Chinese currency was easily identified with the creation of offshore financial markets on which renminbi securities were traded (**3.**).

1. The smiling face of the "Great Helmsman"

The People's Bank of China has been responsible for the design, printing and issuance of the RMB since its founding. Today, the legal tender banknotes in the PRC are those of the fifth series (1999), which includes denominations of 1, 5, 10, 20, 50 and 100 yuan and bills of 1, 2 and 5 jiao. Coins of 1 yuan, 5 and 1 jiao, and less frequently 5, 2 and 1 fen are still in circulation.

This fifth series is radically different from the others in that each banknote is illustrated with one portrait, and only one, that of the first president of the PRC (1949-1959)[7] .

The educated son of a wealthy peasant, **Mao Zedong** (毛泽东, 1893-1976) contributed to the founding of the Chinese Communist Party (CCP) in 1921. He established himself in the political bureau in 1935 during the **Long March** (长征, changzheng), at the Zunyi Conference. He officially took the reins of the party on March 20, 1943, and remained General Secretary of the CCP until his death on September 9, 1976.

---

[7] President of the Chinese Central People's Government (from 1er October 1949 to 27 September 1954) then President of the People's Republic of China (from 27 September 1954 to 28 April 1959).

In the vocabulary of the merchant marine, the helmsman is the sailor who holds the tiller, or helm, to ensure the proper direction of a ship. Reinforced by the qualifier of "Great" and the capital letters, the metaphor of **"Great Helmsman"** (伟大的舵手, weida de duoshou), gave its recipient the aura of the guide who knows the way and will bring his people, and thus the Chinese nation, "safely to port." The cult of personality (one man rules China) was accentuated with the **Great Leap Forward** (1958-1960, 大跃进, da yue jin); propaganda thus masking, as seems customary in totalitarian regimes, the failure of the new economic direction, and the famines that followed, by praising the great organizer of industrial and agricultural collectivism. **Chen Boda** (陈伯达, 1904-1989) had appeared to be one of Mao's first flatterers to use the phrase, in August 1966, at the beginning of the **Great Proletarian Cultural Revolution** (无产阶级文化大革命, wuchan jieji wenhua da geming) (1966-1976), galvanizing the manipulated youth to restore the power of the leader challenged by the bureaucracy[8] . The cult of the leader was nurtured early on, as illustrated by the propaganda posters

---

[8] For example, Marshal Peng Dehuai (1898-1974) denounced in an open letter the effects of the Great Leap Forward in the countryside as a radical policy that reflected "petty bourgeois fanaticism". During the Cultural Revolution, he tried to commit suicide after his arrest by the Red Guards.

before the regime's establishment and the parade on October 1, 1959, marking the 10th anniversary of the founding of the PRC, where the crowd chanted **"ten thousand years"**[9] (万岁, wan sui), as in the days of wishing "long life" to the emperor of imperial China. Yet this personalization of power did not appear on banknotes or coins during the Red Emperor's lifetime.

When the printing of the first three denominations (10, 20 and 50 yuan) of the first renminbi series was planned in 1948, before the founding of the regime, there was no doubt in Dong Biwu's and Nan Hanchen's mind that Mao Zedong's portrait should be printed on the new banknotes, in accordance with the Soviet practice or the first denominations issued in the 1930s which featured the "people's representatives". However, the General Secretary of the CCP refused to have his portrait printed because "the banknotes are issued by the government, not by the party"! And when he became president of the Chinese Central People's Government, he repeated his refusal to have his image printed, as well as the use of the names of other leaders or the names of cities.

---

[9] The Emperor was addressed by the title "Lord of Ten Thousand Years" (万岁爷, wansuiye). This term would be found again during the Cultural Revolution (1966-1976), with the term "lord" being replaced by "Chairman Mao" (毛主席万岁, Máo zhuxi wansui).

The inscription of a post-mortem personality cult on monetary signs thus appears both late and "total" since only the "Red Sun", like the color of communism or that of the 100-yuan banknote, has the honor of being handled by more than a billion individuals every day.

The presence of human faces on banknotes is never insignificant. It is one of the elements aimed at reinforcing the national sentiment, and the familiarity of these figures ends up creating what political scientist Benedict Anderson (1936-2015) called the **"imagined community"** (想象中的共同体, xiangxiang zhong de gongtongti). This remark holds for the previous political figures but questions more for the founder of the PRC. Indeed, it is quite surprising that in the 21st century the young and smiling face of the "Great Helmsman" leads China... towards new waters of a state capitalism that, even designated under the official name of a "socialist market economy", remains far from Maoist dreams. It is also comical to note that the author of On Contradiction (1937) is honored by the central bank, even though he had refused to have his portrait printed on banknotes during his lifetime and, in his past as a young revolutionary, wanted to abolish money, as did a number of socialist thinkers who asserted that, in a planned economy, goods should be distributed directly without the intermediary of coins or bills.

To understand what may appear to be a paradox or, in the vocabulary of the Maoists, "right-wing deviationism", let us first point out that the new generations of communist elites in the State Council have mostly ousted his former comrades in arms Zhou Enlai, Liu Shaoqi and Zhu De, who, along with Mao Zedong, had the honors of the 100-yuan bill in the previous series. The only survivor of this symbolic "currency purge", the Red Leader's omnipresence on the fiat currency may seem eternal as his face now appears in mobile applications distributing the new digital yuan. Yet in 2006, representatives of the National People's Congress (NPC) proposed introducing new faces on banknotes: The names of **Deng Xiaoping** (邓小平, 1904-1997), considered the "father" of economic reforms, or **Sun Yat-sen** (孫逸仙 also Sun Zhongshan, 孫中山, 1866-1925), the "father" of the 1911 revolution, whose bust had long illustrated the banknotes of the Republic of China, were put forward, but these proposals were not turned into law.

Since the Great Leader crowded out other political figures, but also agricultural or industrial workers and faces from ethnic minorities, let us put forward a hypothesis: this "total politicization" through the personification of money signs may have been one of the firewalls of the modernizing elites to protect themselves from contestation within the party or even by certain social groups downgraded by the closures of enterprises linked to the liberalization of the economy, layoffs in low-productivity state-owned conglomerates or social plans in over-staffed administrations. In a country committed to reform policies based on the introduction of market mechanisms and the opening up of trade to the outside world, monetary and financial policy is necessarily accompanied by a break with past monetary exchanges. In contrast to the Maoist program of building socialism based on self-sufficiency and mass mobilization, it requires more money in circulation. However, printing Mao's face on the main monetary signs, in a country where citizens forbid themselves any irreverent behavior with the images of the "Great Leader", makes it more difficult to criticize this monetarization of the economy, which is manifested by the multiplication of banknotes. The founder is made sacred in order to mask, like the 100-yuan banknotes of the early 2000s, the violence of the wealth gap between citizens, which is also manifested by the accumulation of monetary signs.

Finally, let us look ahead. When the NPC proposed the names of Sun Yat-sen or Deng Xiaoping, it was because they, along with Mao Zedong, were the only figures mentioned by name in the preamble of the PRC Constitution. With the 5th amendment of March 11, 2018, a new figure can claim monetary cults: that of **Xi Jinping** (习近平, 1953-)[10] .

---

[10] "The various nationalities of China, led by the Chinese Communist Party and guided by Marxism-Leninism, Mao Zedong's thought, Deng Xiaoping's theory, the important principle of the "Three Representations", the scientific concept of development and Xi Jinping's thought on Chinese-style socialism of the new era, will maintain the people's democratic dictatorship, continue on the socialist path, in the policy of reform and opening up to the outside world,..." (Preamble of the Chinese Constitution)

2. Towards limited exchange rate flexibility

An **exchange rate regime** (汇率制度, huilü zhidu) is the set of rules that determine the possible interventions of the monetary authorities in the foreign exchange market, thus the behavior of the exchange rate. A classic distinction is made between **fixed exchange rate regimes** (固定汇率制度, guding huilü zhidu), where the monetary authorities commit to a reference parity between the country's currency and another currency (or basket of currencies) and **flexible exchange rate regimes** (浮动汇率制度, fudong huilü zhidu), where the monetary authorities have made no commitment to maintain the exchange rate of their currency against other currencies, leaving it to be set according to supply and demand in the foreign exchange market. Between these two regimes, **intermediate exchange rate regimes** (中间汇率制, zhongjian huilü zhi) are identified.

If, in the first months of the seizure of power, the exchange rate regime is that of the floating of the new currency; very quickly, the new regime will privilege the fixing of the exchange rate.

The first quotations of the new currency were identified in Tianjin, January 18, 1949 after the control of the former financial center of the north by the soldiers of the People's Liberation Army (PLA). The flight of the Nationalist armies and the sequence of victories did not prevent the devaluation of the currency of an authority engaged in a civil war. The destruction and application of socialist management methods (restricting the movement of goods, controlling markets, seizing the assets of banks and capitalists, physical threats, etc.) did not reassure foreigners about the value of the "people's currency," whose **exchange rate** (汇率, huilü) then registered violent fluctuations against the **United States dollar** (美国美元, meiguo meiyuan or 美元, meiyuan).

Between the years 1949 and 1952, the exchange rate of the RMB was supposed to move on the basis of purchasing power parity; in practice, the external value of the communist regime's currency floated and was further upset by the United Nations embargo during the Korean War (June 25, 1950-July 27, 1953). The new **State Council of the PRC** (中华人民共和国国务院, zhonghua renmin gongheguo guo wu yuan) headed by **Zhou Enlai** (周恩来, 1898-1976), then composed of 15 members and 4 vice-presidents, decided to suspend the publication of the exchange rate with the U.S. dollar in 1952. The government's reference would be the parity with the **pound-sterling** (英镑, yingbang). However, by 1953, the inconvertibility of the currency was decided and exchange controls were drastically imposed. The PRC then had a **fixed exchange rate regime** (固定汇率制度, guding huilü zhidu): the official parity was set at 2.4618 RMB for one U.S. dollar on June 15, 1955. It would remain unchanged despite the economic disasters of the Great Leap Forward (1958-1960), the famines that followed, or the disorganizations of production during the Great Proletarian Cultural Revolution (1966-1976). The five-year plans did little to change the external price of the currency, since between 1955 and 1971 the exchange rate was set at between 2.46 and 2.27 yuan per dollar. And, in a move as obscure as it was unexpected, the government decided, with the end of the Bretton Woods system... to revalue its currency against the dollar. After this new revaluation of the renminbi, the external value against the dollar remained fixed until 1979. Even the deaths of Zhou Enlai and Mao Zedong in January and September 1976 had no effect on the official exchange rate of the Chinese currency. The logic of this exchange rate policy lay in the choice of importing at the lowest possible prices the equipment that would eventually guarantee economic independence.

The reforms initiated under the leadership of **Deng Xiaoping** (邓小平, 1904-1997) involved redefining the rules for setting the external value of the renminbi. Debates on the exchange rate regime of the new China would become increasingly prominent among economic and political elites as the country embarked on a policy of development through export promotion. As a member of the Multi-Fiber Agreement (MFA) in 1983, the PRC obtained permanent observer status in the **General Agreement on Tariffs and Trade** (GATT) (关税和贸易总协定, guanshui he maoyi zong xieding), which was signed on October 30, 1947, to harmonize the customs policies of the signatory parties. After the Tiananmen Square massacres (1989), Chinese diplomacy re-launched discussions on "China's reintegration into the GATT" (1992), especially since Taiwan applied for membership as a separate customs territory. With the establishment of the

World Trade Organization (WTO) (世界商业组织, shijie shangye zuzhi) on 1er January 1995, the Chinese government negotiated to join the new body responsible for establishing rules governing international trade among member countries and settling trade disputes between countries. On December 11, 2001, the People's Republic of China became the 143th member of the WTO[11] . This diplomatic recognition reflects the desire of China, and its trading partners, to promote economic development via insertion into the emerging international division of labor

---

[11] Taiwan joined the organization in January 2002 as the "separate customs territory of Taiwan, Penghu, Kimmen and Matsu".

and **global value chains** (全球价值链, quanqiu jiazhi lian).

The first difficulties in understanding the Chinese exchange rate regime comes from the discrepancy between the official statements of the Chinese government and the (weak) exchange rate developments seen in the market. In short, to use the terminology of the **International Monetary Fund** (IMF) (国际货币基金组织, guoji huobi jijin zuzhi), the differences between the "de jure" exchange rate regime, as declared to the Fund, and the "de facto" one encountered on the foreign exchange market. A long period of exegesis to determine the nature of China's exchange rate regime then began and is still ongoing.

In 1981, the appreciation of the exchange rate was reversed with the depreciation of the Chinese currency against the U.S. dollar for nearly 15 years. In October 1986, the IMF classified the Chinese exchange rate regime as a managed floating exchange rate regime. In fact, the exchange rate has been administered since the 1950s! Nevertheless, the Chinese government defended the idea, in 1991, that its exchange rate regime was primarily a floating regime...

Between 1994 and 2005, the exchange rate remained stable at around 8.28 yuan per dollar for more than eight years (from September 1997 to July 2005).

Note that during the **Asian financial crisis** (亚洲金融危机, yazhou jinrong weiji) and subsequent currency **devaluations** (贬值, bianzhi) in Southeast Asia in September 1997, the People's Bank of China had maintained its exchange rate at 8.28 yuan per dollar when many countries expected it to devalue its currency in order to boost exports. When all its competitors were opting for non-cooperative exchange rate strategies to improve their trade balances, **Zhu Rongji** (朱镕基, 1928-, Prime Minister from March 17, 1998 to March 16, 2003) pledged that the PRC would maintain its parity at 8.28 yuan per dollar, thereby ceding market share to its Asian neighbors but signaling to its trading partners that the Chinese government was an economically responsible ally.

On July 21, 2005, the Chinese government, after a revaluation of 2.1%, resumed the reform undertaken ten years earlier by varying the exchange rate of the RMB within a narrow fluctuation band (± 0.3%) based on a basket of currencies whose content was not made public. In May 2007, the daily fluctuation band of the renminbi against the US dollar was widened from ±0.3% to ±0.5%. With the **2008 global financial crisis** (2008年环球金融危机, 2008 nian huanqiu jinrong weiji), the USD/CNY exchange rate remained at 6.83 yuan per dollar. The PRC again had adopted a quasi-fixed exchange rate regime until mid-June 2010. In July 2010, it reverted to a managed float and the floating band widened to ± 1%.

From the end of 2013, the monetary authorities were committed to minimal intervention in the foreign exchange market. In February 2014, the People's Bank of China depreciated the exchange rate to 6.06 yuan per dollar, and in March, the widening of the daily fluctuation band of the RMB/USD exchange rate to plus or minus 2% gave a greater role to market fluctuations.

In 20 years (1994-2014), the People's Republic of China accompanied the appreciation of the yuan, sometimes, even slowing it down. The exchange rate regime was transformed from a fixed multiple exchange rate regime to a controlled floating regime. However, the choice of exchange rate regime was only a tool to achieve this objective of controlled appreciation.

In its 2014 review, the IMF classified China's exchange rate regime as a "floating or adjustable parity" regime. Moreover, between 2014-2017, the trend was to revalue the yuan against the dollar, despite surprise devaluations. As of 2018, the Chinese exchange rate regime is hardly understood by Fund economists, who put it in residual categories ("other managed arrangement" or "other conventional pegged regimes").

The years 2005-2020 thus marked the gradual abandonment of fixed exchange rates for the Chinese currency against the US currency: flexibility was at the heart of the Chinese agenda. This was confirmed in the following years, as the average exchange rate had fallen from 7.1 yuan per dollar in mid-2020 to 6.3 yuan per dollar in mid-2022.

In 2023, according to the People's Bank of China, the Chinese exchange rate regime is a managed floating regime based on market supply and demand and adjusted against a basket of currencies with a floating band fixed at 2% around the dollar. This "managed floating" regime declared by the Chinese authorities is, in fact, according to the IMF, a crawl-like arrangement.

3. CNY and CNH, currencies of a reforming communist regime

The **renminbi** (人民币), the official currency of the People's Republic of China, is **legal tender** (法定货币, fading huobi) in mainland China. The **yuan** (元) is its monetary unit. Note that the symbol "元" is also used for Japanese and Korean currencies, and it is used to translate the currency units of other countries into Chinese: the **United States dollar** (美元, meiyuan) or American yuan and the **euro** (欧元, ouyuan) or European yuan. The Latinized symbol for the yuan is "¥," which is a capital Y with a double bar although some scripts have only a single horizontal bar ¥ to avoid confusion with the Japanese currency symbol.

According to the International Standard Organization (ISO), the international code (ISO standard 4217) for Chinese currency is CNY (CN for China and Y for yuan). It is sometimes translated as **RMB onshore** (在岸人民币, zai an renminbi).

RMB, CNY and RMB onshore are therefore equivalent, the first acronym being used mainly in the country, the second by players in the international financial markets. For traders, the Chinese currency is sometimes identified by the acronyms CNY SAEC or CNY01, which refer to the spot exchange rate of the RMB with the US dollar for settlement within two business days as it appears on Reuters screens on the SAEC page against the symbol "USD/CNY=" at 5pm Beijing time.

The **internationalization** (国际化, guoji hua) of a currency often involves the development of **offshore financial centers** (离岸金融中心, li an jinrong zhongxin), countries or jurisdictions whose financial institutions conduct numerous transactions with non-residents, in which non-resident agents directly exchange that currency and securities denominated in that currency unit.

In the case of the PRC, the advantages sought in the establishment of an offshore financial center for yuan transactions are not fiscal but aim at controlling the internationalization of its currency.

Offshore renminbi (香港离岸人民币, xianggang li an renminbi), or **CNH**, is renminbi that is traded only outside the mainland. The acronym refers to a currency code invented on the ISO 4217 model to link the abbreviations for China (CN) and Hong Kong (H).

This offshore yuan was inaugurated on July 19, 2010 by the **Hong Kong Monetary Authority (HKMA)** (香港金融管理局, xiangkang jinrong ganli ju or).

The CNH is traded on the Hong Kong interbank market. It is regulated by the HKMA but trading in other financial centers is not prohibited. The CNH, or Hong Kong deliverable renminbi, can be exchanged for any other convertible currency, unlike the renminbi (CNY), which is subject to exchange restrictions since it is not freely deliverable in a forward market and is not fully convertible for capital transactions.

	Control capital		Control capital	
CNH (Asia) *Offshore*		**CNY** *Onshore*		**CNH** (Europe) *Offshore*
Hong Kong				**London**
		Mainland China		
Singapore				**Luxembourg**

The CNH exchange rate is considered to be less controlled by the Chinese central bank and therefore more driven by market forces. In fact, it is more **volatile** (波动, bidong) than the CNY when the same event occurs.

However, these two prices must move in the same direction and experience fluctuations of the same magnitude. This is because the changes in these exchange rates are correlated, as they are linked to Chinese monetary policy expectations. The exchange rates of the US dollar (USD) into the offshore yuan (CNH) and the renminbi (CNY) are therefore close but not always equal.

The Bank of China in Hong Kong (BOCHK) is the leading institution for supplying the interbank market with CNH. It is also the **clearing bank** (清算银行, qinsuan yinhang) for banks that must hold 25% of their customers' cash liabilities.

Note that the CNH is not a new currency! It is the same currency that circulates on the Chinese mainland. It is a renminbi traded in a different market (hence the term "offshore RMB"), with its own regulations and players, and even with a different exchange rate than the mainland renminbi ("onshore RMB").

CHAPTER 3

THE INTERNATIONAL FUTURE AND DIGITAL YUAN

(2016 -)

The assertiveness and professionalism of Chinese diplomacy has allowed the "people's currency" to gain a foothold in international financial institutions (IFIs), including the International Monetary Fund (IMF) (**1.**).

The mastery of digital innovations and a medium-term strategic vision have enabled the People's Republic of China (PRC) to become the first economic power to issue a central bank digital currency (CBD) on a large scale (**2.**).

The development of new financial technologies and the ambitions of the Chinese government are having an impact on the international financial system. They call into question the supremacy of the dollar in the international monetary system (IMS) (**3.**).

The People's Republic of China (PRC) had remained wary of the multilateral economic institutions that welcomed the Republic of China (Taiwan) for a long time. However, it began a turnaround in 1971 that would accelerate in the late 1970s, with the policy of reform and opening up launched by **Deng Xiaoping** (邓小平, 1904-1997). On October 25, 1971, the 26th session of the United Nations General Assembly adopted Decision No. 2758, which integrated the communist state into the United Nations. On November 15, a delegation led by **Qiao Guanhua** (乔冠华, 1913-1983) attended the General Assembly of the world's leading forum for the first time which no longer included the world's most populous country!

The Articles of Agreement of the International Monetary Fund (IMF) and the World Bank were drafted at the International Monetary and Financial Conference in Bretton Woods, New Hampshire, USA in July 1944. The Republic of China (1912-1949) was one of the 44 signatory countries that wanted to establish a framework for economic cooperation to ensure the stability of the international monetary system. The Fund began operations with a \$25 million loan to France. The founding of the People's Republic of China would only slowly change the governance of these international financial institutions. Nearly thirty-five years later, the Executive Board of the International Monetary Fund (IMF) recognized the PRC as a member country, responding to a request from the Chinese authorities which had been expressed since the mid-1970s. By becoming a member of the international financial institution in 1980[12] , the PRC won a new diplomatic battle; however, membership in the Fund was not the primary objective of the Chinese authorities, although the recovery of China's foreign exchange and gold assets was an opportunity, as was the possibility of benefiting from the Fund's financing instruments[13] . Nonetheless, the key for the PRC was to join the **World Bank Group** (世界银行集团, shijie yinhang jituan), which provides access to low-

---

[12] Here, Taiwan is excluded from the IMF (unlike the WTO), but the Fund publishes Taiwan's data under the name "Taiwan Province of China".

[13] The People's Republic of China (PRC) will benefit from the International Monetary Fund's Stand-By Arrangements. Established in June 1952, the IMF's Stand-By Arrangement (SBA) is a lending instrument with an average maturity of 12 to 24 months to help countries to overcome balance of payments problems in the event of an economic crisis. In March 1981, for an amount of SDR 450 million, and then in November 1986, for SDR 597.7 million, the PRC acceded to this lending instrument.

interest loans, via the International Development Agency, for developing countries.

In October 1950, Nan Hanchen, the first governor of the People's Bank of China, had written to the president of the **International Bank for Reconstruction and Development** (IBRD) （国际复兴开发银行, guoji fuxing kaifa yinhang) that China's rights to the financing bank belonged to "the Chinese people," and thus to the PRC. This claim is now accompanied by fund-raising for new development programs.

Today, the IMF has two main missions: to promote international monetary cooperation and to foster the expansion of international trade and economic growth. As part of this, **special drawing rights** (SDRs) （特别提款权, tebie ti kuan quan) were created in 1969. Their values were expressed in gold. After the end of the Bretton Woods system (1971), the composition of the SDR changed to include the currencies of growing countries that had taken a significant share in exports of goods and services. In 1981, the number of currencies in the SDR basket was reduced from sixteen to five: the U.S. dollar, the Japanese yen, the German mark, the British pound and the French franc. In 1999, the euro replaced the two euro-zone currencies (German mark and French franc) and the SDR became a basket of four currencies.

Thirty years after joining the Fund, the PRC, supported by Russia, India and Brazil, entered the governing bodies of the international financial institution (IFI). On July 26, 2011, the former vice-governor of the People's Bank of China who had started his career at the Bank of China (BOC), **Zhu Min**[14] （朱民, 1952) was appointed Deputy Managing Director of the IMF by Christine Lagarde, who had just created this new ad hoc position. This appointment (2011-2016) allowed both of them to give emerging countries a more important role within the institution and to satisfy the PRC, whose economic weight was growing and whose financial diplomacy no longer hid the desire to bypass the IFIs stemming from Bretton Woods. In addition, the creation of this post also made it possible to bypass the blocking of Japan and to offer Asia two of the main management positions. Today, five years after this appointment, the

---

[14] Born in 1952, in Shanghai, Zhu Min （朱民, 1952) was a teenager during the Cultural Revolution (1966-1976). He would be forced to drop out of high school and work as a truck driver in a cannery until 1977. The reopening of university admissions allowed him to be admitted to the Department of Economics at Fudan University in 1982. After graduating with a bachelor's degree in economics, he studied in the United States from 1985, earning a master's degree in public administration from the Woodrow Wilson School of Public and International Affairs at Princeton University, and a master's degree in applied economics and a doctorate in economics from Johns Hopkins University. Zhu Min is the first national of the People's Republic of China to be appointed Deputy Managing Director of the International Monetary Fund (2011-2016).

RMB is one of the five currencies forming the SDR basket.

Since 2015, the currencies that make up the SDR basket had to be "freely usable", "widely used to settle international transactions" and "commonly traded in major foreign exchange markets". The renminbi (RMB) was recognized by the IMF Executive Board as possessing these three qualities. It could therefore be included in the basket. The formula for weighting a currency took into account the value of exports of goods and services over the previous five years as well as financial data (official reserves held by other monetary authorities, volume of foreign exchange transactions, outstanding international banking liabilities, etc.).

On October 1st 2016, the International Monetary Fund (IMF) Special Drawing Rights (SDR) currency basket was expanded to include the RMB as a fifth currency. The renminbi, now considered a **"freely usable"** currency （可自由使用, ke ziyou shiyong), was the fifth currency with a weighting of 10.92%, alongside the US dollar (41.73%), the euro (30.93%), the yen (8.33%), and the British pound (8.09%). The value of the SDR would be equal to the sum of the values of the amounts of each currency: 0.58252 US dollars, 0.38671 euros, 1.0174 yuan, 11900 yen and 0.085946 pounds sterling. The SDR interest rate would reflect this new SDR basket by including a representative interest rate for the renminbi.

For Christine Lagarde, then Managing Director of the IMF, this was "an important and historic milestone for the SDR, the IMF, China and the international monetary system". First, because it was the first time since the adoption of the euro that a currency was added to the basket. Second, because the inclusion of the Chinese currency reflected the change in the PRC's diplomatic and financial status. Finally, because the Fund, which was often criticized on this point, was giving a larger place to an emerging country in the international monetary and financial system. The search for diplomatic prestige was not unequivocal. The inclusion of the RMB in the SDR basket had strengthened the IMF in the face of criticism of its governance and its slowness to give a larger place to the great emerging powers of Africa and Asia.

The latest revision of the SDR valuation method on 1st August 2022 confirmed and strengthened the status of international reserve currency as China's weight in world trade was growing. Two perspectives had framed the reflection since the first evaluation of the weight of the RMB in the SDR currency basket, the first one focused on the performance at a given moment (weight in world trade, in capital flows, etc.). The second focused less on the weight at a given moment than on the stability of performance. From both points of view, the weight of the renminbi must be strengthened. It therefore rose from 10.92% to 12.28% behind the US dollar (43.38%) and the euro (29.31%), but ahead of the yen (7.59%) and the pound sterling (7.44%).

The inclusion of the RMB in the SDR basket renewed the debate on reserve assets and their management by the monetary authorities.

Reserve assets (外汇储备, waihui chubei) are "those external assets that are readily available and controlled by the monetary authorities to meet balance of payments financing needs, to intervene in foreign exchange markets, to influence the exchange rate, and for other related purposes (such as maintaining confidence in the currency and the economy, and serving as a basis for external borrowing)." These foreign reserves are therefore made up of foreign assets that are immediately available to the national authorities, such as monetary gold, special drawing rights (SDRs), the reserve position in the IMF, foreign currency and other claims.

The People's Republic of China (PRC) is the world's largest holder of foreign exchange reserves, with nearly $3.5 trillion in foreign exchange reserves in 2022. These holdings are mainly composed of U.S. Treasury bills. In the same year, the PRC held more than $10 billion in IMF reserve positions and $51.3 billion in SDRs. It should be noted that the Chinese central bank is also a major holder of gold, with more than \$107 billion in official gold reserves in 2022. If at the beginning of the reforms, the country was characterized by a foreign currency debt, the accumulation of trade surpluses from the 1990s onwards would lead to a rapid increase in these reserves, which reached a peak of almost 4,300 billion dollars in 2013.

In the face of such amounts, the PRC appears to be as tied to the stability of the US currency as the US Treasury. Moreover, **State Administration of Foreign Exchange (SAFE)** (国家外汇管理局, guojia waihui guanli ju) does not set much of an example on diversifying foreign exchange reserves.

Nevertheless, the inclusion of the RMB in SDRs encourages central banks to include the Chinese currency in their foreign reserves to diversify their reserve asset structures. Sovereign and non-sovereign investors alike are looking to the RMB bond market for a supply of securities that offer good yields and greater safety than those of other emerging economies. PRC and Chinese state-owned bank bonds can offer such safe investments with high yields, especially as the liquidity of securities and money market instruments have improved. In addition, expectations of an appreciating RMB increase the yield outlook.

In this area, the attitude of sovereign monetary authorities varies widely from one country to another. Central banks can stay away from this new international currency like the US Federal Reserve or buy RMB securities directly on the mainland bond market like the Chilean monetary authority. Most central banks are implementing procedures that facilitate the use of the RMB for invoicing and settling commercial and financial transactions of the country's economic actors, or are carrying out some operations for diplomatic purposes or to monitor the evolution of the regulatory landscape.

The **European Central Bank** (ECB) (欧洲中央银行, ouzhou zhongyang yinhang) placed part of its foreign reserves in yuan after the inclusion of the renminbi (RMB) in the SDR. The RMB thus meets the criteria of liquidity, security and yield that the ECB requires in managing its foreign exchange reserves. Admittedly, the 500 million euros invested in 2017 represented about 1% of the European Central Bank's foreign exchange reserves, but after the Swiss National Bank; the ECB is therefore the second monetary authority of an advanced economy to diversify its reserves with the Chinese currency. Its foreign reserve portfolio now consists of US dollars, Japanese yen, gold, special drawing rights and renminbi.

This cautious attitude contrasts with that of other monetary authorities, particularly in developing countries. For example, the Central Bank of Chile (BCCh) had extensive relations with Chinese monetary authorities well before the inclusion of the RMB in SDRs. The Banco central de Chile's first offshore RMB deposits were made in 2010, and then the Chilean monetary authority obtained permission from the People's Bank of China to invest in the onshore market with a quota of CNY 2,600 million. In 2015, the BCCh invested directly in onshore bonds. In 2015, the two central banks signed a bilateral renminbi/Chilean peso swap agreement. In August 2021, the bilateral agreement was renewed for a period of 5 years. The amount of the swap line was increased from RMB 22 billion to RMB 50 billion, which is about 7.1 billion US dollars (USD). The requested funds, if any, are to be used to facilitate foreign trade operations between Chile and China or contribute to the stability of financial markets. In 2018, the Chilean central bank engaged in a partnership with the Industrial and Commercial Bank of China (ICBC) to operate on its behalf in the onshore fixed income market.

A **liquidity arrangement** (流动性安排, liudong xing anpai) provides liquidity in a currency through a system of reserve pooling by participating central banks. The Chilean central bank diversifies its liquidity arrangements via RMB investment pools set up by the People's Bank of China and the **Bank for International Settlements** (BIS) （国际清算银行, guoji qingsuan yinhang). The BIS is an international organization that promotes international monetary and financial cooperation and acts as a bank for its 63-member monetary authorities. Within this framework, it acts as a depository agent for guarantees in international financial transactions. Thus, the **RMB Liquidity Arrangement** (RMBLA) （人民币流动性安排, renminbi liudong xing anpai) provides foreign exchange through a system of reserve pooling by the participating central banks. The purpose is to provide lines of credit, particularly in times of market volatility. Note that in the agreement signed with the People's Bank of China in June 2022, reserve pooling allows certain monetary authorities (Bank Indonesia, Central Bank of Malaysia, Hong Kong Monetary Authority, Monetary Authority of Singapore, Central Bank of Chile), which contribute a minimum of 15 billion renminbi (RMB) or the equivalent in US dollars (USD), to draw on their contributions and also to have access to additional financing through a guaranteed liquidity window managed by the BIS. Thus, for the Chilean authorities, the aim is to obtain, in addition to international reserves, the possibility of participating in an alternative mechanism for providing funds in exceptional situations. The delivery of instruments denominated in renminbi becomes a guarantee... like liquidity in US dollars.

The share of Chinese securities in the reserves of the Central Bank of Chile (BCCh) has risen from 2% to 8% in a decade, illustrating that the **renminbization** (人民币化, renminbi hua) of central bank balance sheets can be rapid. This dynamic is also found in larger economies. For example, the South African Reserve Bank (SARB) has been investing in the onshore bond market since 2013, before the inclusion of the RMB in SDRs, and has increased the size of its RMB allocation twice since then. In 2015, the SARB signed a three-year bilateral swap agreement with the People's Bank of China for 30 billion yuan ($4.5 billion). It was renewed in 2018. In July 2015, the Bank of China's (BOC) Johannesburg branch became the first RMB **clearing bank** (清算银行, qinsuan yinhang) in Africa for private players. It allows for direct yuan settlements without the need for an intermediate currency, similar to the US dollar. In June 2016, the Chinese and South African central banks and the **China Foreign Exchange Trade System** (CFETS) (中国外汇交易中心, zhongguo waihui jiaoyi zhongxin) agreed to allow direct trade between the renminbi (RMB) and rand

(ZAR) on the Chinese interbank foreign exchange market to reduce conversion costs between the two currencies and promote bilateral trade or investment. The South African rand and Chinese renminbi can therefore be traded in the Chinese interbank market on a bilateral basis. A month later, the South African central bank conducted its first direct RMB bond transaction with the BOC as the direct counterparty in the Chinese interbank bond market. Converging with the South African diplomatic call for greater cooperation among the BRICS, the central bank is diversifying its foreign exchange reserves through RMB bonds, both onshore and offshore. The RMB is therefore one of the 14 currencies eligible for inclusion in the SARB's foreign exchange reserves and would be the third currency in its reserves with a weighting of 13%.

Along with Angola, Ghana, Kenya, Nigeria and Tanzania, South Africa is a testament to the wider use of the Chinese currency in trade and investment between China and Africa, as in other parts of the world. Nearly 30 monetary authorities hold RMB as a reserve currency, and there is a general trend toward increasing central bank involvement in the currency. This movement has been reinforced by the "weaponization of the dollar", the use of the US currency and US-controlled market infrastructure for foreign policy purposes. For example, the freezing of Russia's foreign exchange reserves by the United States and its allies after its renewed invasion of Ukraine in

February 2022 has prompted countries potentially subject to western economic sanctions to diversify their foreign exchange reserves.

By holding foreign exchange reserves in RMB, the monetary authorities are strengthening the role of the Chinese currency in the regulation of exchange rates and global liquidity. Of course, there are still many challenges. On the Chinese mainland, they can be seen both in the structure of the financial markets and in the procedures for trading securities. Moreover, the opening of the country to all capital flows is still to come for a wider internationalization of the RMB. Not to mention the issue of payment infrastructure or flexible exchange rate. According to the Financial Times, by the end of 2021 less than 3% of foreign exchange reserves were invested in renminbi but this share is growing.

2. The e-yuan, a central bank digital currency (CBDC)

At the end of the 13th century, European readers of **Marco Polo** (马可.波罗, 1254-1324) discovered in the Devisements on the World (1298) one of the "wonders" encountered by the young Venetian in the empire of **Kubilai Khan** (忽必烈, 1215-1294), who possessed an "alchemy" that allowed him to hold "more wealth than all the kings on earth." The bills are a Chinese invention and the nephew of European merchants who entered the service of the Mongol emperor to specify that "The Great Khan uses these bills to pay what he owes. All his provinces, kingdoms and lands must use them, as well as his subjects, wherever he has power and authority. No one, as long as he values his life, dares to refuse them, as he would be immediately punished with death. Besides, all accept them willingly."

Today, the astonishment that strikes tourists, students or expatriate executives in China is no longer the appearance but the disappearance of banknotes in major metropolises! Indeed, to pay a small commercial debt, to rent a property or to buy a simple dish from a street vendor, the QR code reader on one's cell phone is the most common payment vector. In the 21st century, in the **Middle Kingdom** (中国, zhong guo), digital transactions have spread as quickly as the horse troops of Mongolian armies, and the "tumultuous movement" now is that of chats on social networks, clicks on e-commerce sites, ratings on sharing platforms or codes generated by online payment apps.

The **digital revolution** (数字革命, shuzi geming) is also a monetary disruption, and the People's Bank of China, like the majority of central banks, is being pushed around by the digitization of currency signs. However, while nearly 70 monetary authorities have embarked on **digital currency** (数字货币, shuzi huobi) projects, China's central bank has stood out from the majority of its peers in terms of **agility** (敏捷, minjie). As early as 2014, the People's Bank of China had included the development of such a tool in its agenda. Six years later, it conducted the first pilot tests... in the city that was the laboratory of economic revival in 1978.

A **Central Bank Digital Currency** (CBDC) (中央银行数字货币, zhongyang yinhang shuzi huobi), is a dematerialized payment instrument, denominated in the national unit of account and directly representing a liability due from the central bank. CBDC is therefore additional to the other forms of money issued by a monetary authority: coins and banknotes as well as the electronic deposits, or reserves, of commercial banks with the central bank.

The Bank for International Settlements (BIS), defines a CBDC as "a central bank liability, denominated in an existing unit of account, that serves both as a medium of exchange and as a store of value". It calls for a distinction to be made between the issuance of a :

- wholesale CBDCs, available only to financial intermediaries;

- retail CBDCs, accessible to the general public.

Since the two issues can be separated, a central bank can manage one or two CBDCs. The motivations of central banks for issuing these CBDCs are varied.

The main motive for issuing a wholesale CBDC today is to promote financial innovation and lower transaction costs, especially via mastering **blockchain technologies**[15] (区块链技术, qu kuai lian jishu). The main reason for issuing a retail CBDC is to provide economic agents with "a dematerialized monetary instrument that is free of liquidity or credit risk, easy to access and inexpensive."

The People's Bank of China has issued a retail CBDC, the **e-yuan** (or **e-CNY**). This new payment instrument is intended to eventually replace banknotes and coins in circulation, as it will be a legal tender.

---

[15] Blockchain technology is a technology for storing and transmitting information in the form of a database.

However, it is not intended to replace cashless money deposited in bank accounts.

Moreover, commercial banks have a role to play in the distribution of China's digital currency since the e-yuan takes the form of **Digital Currency/Electronic Payment** (or DC/EP) (数字货币电子支付, shuzi huobi dianzi zhifu). Indeed, this retail digital currency is a two-tiered design:

- 1st level, the central bank controls the digital currency (DC);

- at the second level, the electronic payment platforms (EP) participate in the system, alongside the banks, as intermediaries for consumers and companies.

For a country like the PRC, this innovation can fit both into the desire to ensure financial stability, provide modern governance that strengthens the CCP's legitimacy... and better control the population even though the government claims to guarantee **"controllable anonymity"** (可控匿名, ke kong niming), which means the People's Bank of China retains full supervision over the digital currency but grants users a certain amount of anonymity for their transactions and protection of their personal information from other third parties. Full anonymity will not be implemented via this DC/EP in order to deter crimes and misdemeanors such as tax evasion, terrorist financing and money laundering, according to the monetary authorities.

The PRC is continuing its work on digitizing currency by expanding pilot areas, deepening uses and improving system security. For example, in the trials, users can withdraw their e-yuan (or e-CNY) from ATMs or e-wallets on their smartphones and can conduct these transactions without an Internet connection. They do not need to be linked to a bank account... only a phone number.

The e-yuan is not a **crypto asset** (加密资产, jiami zichan), like **bitcoin** (比特币, bite bi). Moreover, it does not rely on blockchain technology. We have forgotten it, but Venezuela remains the first state to offer a "sovereign crypto asset" in 2018, the Petro (PTR). In the words of the Maduro government, the digital asset presented itself as "spearheading the development of an independent digital economy, transparent and open to direct citizen participation." Beyond seeking new legitimacy and funds via technology, the initiative was unique in using Venezuela's oil assets and blockchain technology to promote the adoption of a crypto asset. One reason for its failure is that the value of the **token** (代币, daibi) was supported by oil resources, part of which is already sold forward... to China.

The speed with which the CD/EP was developed can be explained by the long-term vision of Chinese financial leaders and the skills that the government was able to mobilize. The development of the digital yuan involved the state's top hierarchy, notably the Financial Stability and Development Committee, and public and private technology groups, including:

- the major state-owned commercial banks, namely the Bank of China (BOC), China Construction Bank (CCB), Agricultural Bank of China (ABC), Industrial and Commercial Bank of China (ICBC), Bank of Communications (Bocom) and the Post Office Bank of China (PSB);

- Communication groups such as China Mobile, China Telecom, China Unicom;

- Payment companies such as China UnionPay;

- digital groups, especially their subsidiaries specializing in **financial technologies** (金融科技, jinrong keji) or fintech such as Ant Group, a subsidiary of Alibaba Group (Alipay), Tencent (WeChat Pay), Huawei Technologies, etc.

Monetary authorities have also benefited from one of the idiosyncrasies of the Chinese market in which many consumers have moved directly from cash payments to mobile payments. QR codes and digital wallets have become the gateways to **financial inclusion** (普惠金融, pu hui jinrong).

The interest of e-yuan is not only internal. The low transaction costs and ease of payment could provide a cheaper and more convenient alternative in many international transactions. Therefore, the rise of China's digital currency should also be thought of in the context of the transformations of the **international monetary system** (IMS) (国际货币体系, guoji huobi tixi).

3. The renminbi, the tomb of the US dollar?

The People's Republic of China (PRC) is not the first state to develop a cryptocurrency. The sand dollar, a digital version of the **Bahamian dollar** (BSD) (巴哈马元, bahama yuan) issued by the Central Bank of the Bahamas in collaboration with private financial institutions, is chronologically the first central bank digital currency (CBDC). Nevertheless, the Chinese initiative has a different dimension and scope than that of the Bahamian dollar, which is intended to attract new technology companies to its territory. With the digital yuan, the People's Bank of China is taking a lead over the central banks of other economic powers.

China's monetary advance reignites the controversy over the future of the U.S. dollar as the dominant international currency. Moreover, with the digital yuan perceived as a "national security issue," U.S. monetary authorities have accelerated the **digital dollar** (数字美元, shuzi meiyuan) project. In November 2022, the New York Federal Reserve launched a 12-week operation to test the "technical feasibility and legal and commercial viability" of a digital currency in collaboration with banking and financial groups (Citi, HSBC, Wells Fargo, Mastercard, etc.).

In general, the People's Bank of China and Chinese financial technology companies seem to be taking a technological lead in **cryptographic** processes (密碼學, mima xue) that are disrupting traditional **payment systems** (支付系统, zhifu xitong). Its "pilot tests" contrast with the procrastination of U.S. monetary authorities, who have just put the brakes on a private **stable coin** (稳定币, wending bi) project, or token indexed to one or more of Facebook's currencies (Libra and then Diem), and are finding it difficult to reach a consensus on the regulations that need to be established in these sectors.

But the technologies that are shaping the financial landscape are also shaking up the geopolitical order, as illustrated by the **Society for Worldwide Interbank Financial Telecommunications** (环球银行间金融 通信协会, huanqiu yinghang jian jinrong tongxin xiehui) or SWIFT financial messaging network. The U.S.-controlled Belgian cooperative company enables fast international financial transactions. It has established itself through its technological capabilities and legal framework, which allow millions of standardized financial messages to be exchanged every day in more than 200 countries or territories.

At a time when the US dollar and SWIFT worry many countries, often authoritarian regimes, that question the legitimacy of the United States, and more broadly Western countries, to take advantage of the current systems and apply financial sanctions, technological alternatives for international financial transactions are welcome for countries that want to avoid extra-territoriality (US law automatically applies to transactions made in US dollars, regardless of the country), unilateral sanctions (fines, embargoes, seizures, etc.) decided by the executive branch against companies or states and retroactive effects of US law decided by the executive branch against companies or states and the retroactive effects of US law.

A currency can be defined by its functions, an **international currency** (国际货币, guoji huobi) serves both as a unit of account for trade billings between countries, as an intermediary in international trade or financial transactions, and as a store of value for its non-resident holders.

The status of the U.S. dollar is explained by both the economic weight of the United States and its **capital markets** (资本市场, ziben shichang) that remain **deep** (深度, shendu) and **liquid** (流动性, liudong xing). Moreover, the habits of international players reduce

transaction costs (交易成本, jiaoyi chengben), amplify **economies of scale** (规模经济, guimo jingji), generate **positive externalities** (正外部性, zheng waibu xing) and **network effects** (网络效应, wangluo xiaoying) that strengthen the international position of the U.S. dollar, which dominates the renminbi in all functions of an international currency.

Thus, the dollar remains the main currency:

- in currency pairs traded in the foreign exchange market.

More broadly, it remains the **anchor currency** (锚定货币, mao ding huobi) of the international monetary system:

- in international commercial and financial transactions;
- in the foreign exchange reserves of central banks.

Nevertheless, the "people's currency" is nibbling away at the positions of the US currency in all these areas.

As the largest producer and the largest consumer of gold since 2013, the PRC launched its yuan gold quotation system in April 2016. Today, the precious metal is priced in London in U.S. dollars and on the **Shanghai Gold Exchange** (SGE) (上海黄金交易所, Shanghai huangjin jiaoyi suo), where a quotation system establishes a yuan price twice a day.

After yellow gold, black gold! In 2022, Saudi Arabia, the world's largest oil producer, which buys a quarter of its production from China, committed itself to billing the PRC for oil sold in yuan. This "small change" has important consequences. First, it has symbolic significance. Oil market prices have long been set in US dollars, confirming its status as an international unit of account. Second, it may have broader practical implications if the Saudi move is followed by the Gulf Cooperation Council (GCC) countries.

The term **petroyuans** (石油元, shiyou yuan) will then not be confined to Aramco's sales brochures but could become part of the vocabulary of international finance.

Already in 2017, oil pricing in yuan was at the heart of discussions between the People's Bank of China and the Central Bank of the Russian Federation. The adoption of the yuan as the unit of account for these transactions in international markets could also expand to Iran and Venezuela. Moreover, this dynamic could be accelerated if future contracts in this market are also denominated in yuan[16] .

---

[16] Since March 2018, the Shanghai Futures Exchange (SHFE) (上海期货交易所, Shanghai qihuo jiaoyi suo), Shanghai's international energy exchange, offers commodity futures and options, has introduced yuan oil trading.

Thus, if only 10% of global transactions are recorded in yuan, the "de-dollarization" of international markets is no longer a hypothesis, it is a trend!

This trend is reinforced by the efforts of Chinese diplomacy towards its Asian neighbors or within the BRICS.

Indeed, the PRC is encouraging Asian countries to trade in their respective currencies in order to promote invoicing and payments in renminbi. In addition, it is setting up financial institutions that aim to strengthen its weight in the region like the **Asian Infrastructure Investment Bank** (**AIIB**) (亚洲基础设施投资银行 － 亚投行, yazhou jichu sheshi touzi yinhang - ya touhang), headquartered in Beijing. This development bank aims to promote sustainable economic development and improve infrastructure connectivity in Asia.

The term **BRICS** (金砖国家, jin zhuan guojia) is the acronym for five countries-Brazil, Russia, India, China and South Africa. These five emerging powers claim "a stable, predictable and more diversified currency system" and, more broadly, a more important place in international organizations. This new club of powers has established the **New Development Bank** (**NDB**) (新开发银行, xin kaifa yinghang, or 金砖国家开发银行, jin zhuan guojia kaifa yinhang for BRICS Development Bank), headquartered in Shanghai. The NBD is an international financial institution that aims to strengthen financial cooperation among the BRICS and complement multilateral and regional financial institutions. NBD loans to countries that request them are denominated in local currency.

More broadly, the **Silk Road Fund** (丝路基金, si lu jijin), an investment structure established on December 29, 2014, aims to support the "One Belt and One Road" initiatives proposed by the People's Republic of China to enhance its cooperation with countries in Asia, Europe and Africa. The company will mainly invest in infrastructure, industrial and financial cooperation and resource development. The fund is open to both Chinese and foreign investors. While the Silk Road Fund is currently financed mainly by the foreign currency reserves of the China Investment Corporation, China Export-Import Bank and China Development Bank, it can easily promote the use of Chinese currency in development financing.

In December 2020, former People's Bank of China governor **Zhou Xiaochuan** (周小川, 1948) asserted that the digital yuan will not disrupt the order of the global monetary system. He presented the DC/EP as a purely domestic digital currency electronic payment initiative. However, many commentators emphasized that it is also intended to promote cross-border trade and enhance the international status of the yuan. For example, the Australian Strategic Policy Institute, a think tank funded by the Australian Department of Defense, anticipates that the Chinese government "will require foreigners to also use the digital yuan for certain categories of cross-border renminbi transactions, as a condition of access to the Chinese market. This may seem extreme... but it has become plausible.

If the RMB is not the tomb of the dollar, the international rise of the "people's currency" reinforces the hypothesis of a **multipolar monetary system** (多极世界, duo ji shijie) being organized with the rise of the Chinese currency. And in this new multipolar world, the **Eye of Providence**[17] (普罗维登斯之眼, pu luo wei deng si zhi yan) will have to look closely at Chairman Mao's digitized smile.

---

[17] The engraving of an eye placed in a triangle also appears on the back of the U.S. dollar bill and on the Great Seal of the United States.

Yi Gang (易纲, 1958-), the governor of the People's Bank of China since March 19, 2018, usually ends his speeches with a reminder that "in the future, the People's Bank of China will continue to take Xi Jinping's thought on socialism with Chinese characteristics as its guide and implement the guiding principles set forth by the XXᵉ CPC National Congress."

The idea of an independent central bank has no relevance in the PRC and monetary policy is just one of the tools serving the ambition of a president, and a party, who revised the constitution in 2018 to entrench and extend the power of **Xi Jinping** (习近平, 1953-) in order to "achieve the renewal of the Chinese nation."

In 2022, the 20th National Congress of the Communist Party of China confirmed the PRC's new development paradigm based on the **dual domestic and international circuit** (国内国际双循环, guonei guoji shuang xunhuan) or **dual circulation**[18] . The term refers

---

[18] Dual circulation marks an inflection with the "great international circulation" (国际大循环) (Wang Jian, 1987), a development policy that championed the opening up of coastal areas through the development of a manufacturing industry geared toward the export of cheap, low-skilled labor-intensive products.

to an economic policy strategy to simultaneously stimulate the domestic market (domestic circulation) and the external market (international circulation). Domestic circulation focuses on domestic demand and the upgrading of Chinese industry through technological innovation. However, it must be based on the international division of labor and commercial and financial cooperation (cf. foreign investment, technology transfer, etc.) because external resources (capital, technology, know-how, etc.) remain indispensable for the upmarket production of goods and services for internal and external markets. In the development model based on "dual circulation", domestic and foreign markets are mutually reinforcing. And structural reforms on the supply side make it possible to expand domestic and foreign demand.

This strategy entails internal changes but also transformations in globalization in which the PRC, and its currency, are expected to play a more important role. It is therefore not surprising that Vice Premier **Liu He** (刘鹤, 1952-), director of the CCP's Central Commission for Financial and Economic Affairs and Xi Jinping's advisor on economic affairs since 2013, calls for "economic re-globalization" in his January 2023 Davos speech.

These last years have been years of ruptures, in monetary matters as in other fields since the Covid-19 pandemic and the confinements have accelerated the mutations in our ways of consuming, of working, of studying, of meeting... but also of paying. Western countries have become aware of the Chinese lead in digital currency. The CD/EP is not a crypto asset, like Petro or Bitcoin, it is a centralized and sovereign currency.

An innovation is never neutral. This new payment technology could accelerate changes in payments, first within the country, by disrupting the traditional intermediaries that are commercial banks, and between countries, by questioning the efficiency and cost of traditional **payment systems** (支付系统, zhifu xitong) within the global financial architecture. The United States and the People's Republic of China are not just commercial competitors. They are engaged in a power struggle whose stakes are indiscriminately diplomatic, military, economic, technological, financial, monetary, etc. The Chinese CD/EP can therefore be integrated into this framework.

Russia's renewed invasion of Ukraine in February 2022 and the subsequent Western financial sanctions also underscored two important points: that the condemnation of Russia was not unanimous around the world, and that authoritarian regimes are seeking alternatives to the dominance of the U.S. dollar and Western-controlled international payment systems in order to escape financial sanctions, if any.

Prior to his appointment as IMF vice president, **Li Bo**[19] (李波, 1972-), vice governor of the People's Bank of China stated that "the goal is not to replace the U.S. dollar or other international currencies." However, he remained tight-lipped about the Chinese government's international ambitions for its currency.

What is certain is that the "people's currency" is no longer the fragile currency of the early days of communism, which feared being destabilized by its neighbors. It is no longer the currency that could be satisfied with internal objectives, namely fighting hyperinflation and limiting strong price variations. It is no longer the currency that

---

[19] **Li Bo** (李波, 1972 -) graduated from Renmin University of China (Beijing) in 1992 with a bachelor's degree in international economics. He also studied in the United States, where he graduated from Boston University with a master's degree in economics, Stanford University with a doctorate in economics, and Harvard Law School with a doctorate in professional law in August 1999. He began his career at the New York law firm of Davis Polk & Wardwell and then became a partner in the Hong Kong office of Davy & Davy. In August 2018, he became politically involved as the Vice President of the Federation of Overseas Chinese Returnees. He then worked in various positions at the People's Bank of China, where he was appointed deputy governor in April 2021. He was also deputy mayor of Chongqing since 2019, in charge of the development of the city's financial sector, international trade and its foreign direct investment. On August 23, 2021, Li Bo took office as deputy managing director of the IMF and became the third Chinese vice president after **Zhu Min** (朱民, 1952-) and **Zhang Tao** (张涛, 1963-).

shared its function as an intermediary in trade with a multitude of supply vouchers. It is no longer the currency that exporters and importers sought to get rid of as soon as it was acquired. It is no longer the simple vector of monetization of a society that is developing and accessing mass consumption. It is no longer a simple monetary sign whose value depends solely on an internal legitimacy based on the aura of the figure of the regime's founder. It has become one of the five currencies in the IMF's SDR basket and, most importantly, to quote Gita Gopinath (1971-), Deputy Managing Director of the IMF, the **renminbi** (**RMB**) (人民币) is a currency that "aspires to become a global currency".